MEAL PREP COOKBOOK

FOR WEIGHT LOSS

A Complete Guide to Losing Weight While Saving Time and Efforts Through 36 Delicious, Wholesome and Healthy Meal Recipes to Prep and Go

Table of Contents

INTRODUCTION

Various food varieties go through various metabolic pathways in your body. They can have tremendously various impacts on your yearning, chemicals and the quantity of calories you consume.

Getting thinner is to be sure a muddled cycle and it requires better choice of diet plan. This book contains recipes which have low carbs and are productive and powerful in weight decrease. Following are the things which ought to be eaten on the off chance that you need to get more fit

- Eggs are very filling and supplement thick. Contrasted with refined carbs like bagels, eggs can smother craving later in the day and may even advance weight reduction.
- Verdant greens are a magnificent expansion to your weight reduction diet. In addition to the fact that they are low in calories high in fiber that helps keep you feeling full.
- Salmon is high in both protein and omega-3 unsaturated fats, settling on it a decent decision for a solid weight reduction diet.

- Cruciferous vegetables are low in calories yet high in fiber and supplements. Adding them to your eating routine isn't just a phenomenal weight reduction system however may likewise improve your general wellbeing.
- Eating natural lean meat is an amazing method to expand your protein admission. Supplanting a portion of the carbs or fat in your eating regimen with protein could make it simpler for you to lose abundance fat.
- Beans and legumes are a good addition to your weight loss diet. They're both high in protein and fiber, contributing to feelings of fullness and a lower calorie intake.

Meals recipes for weight loss

35 + recipes

1.   15-Minute Korean Beef Bowl

Prep time 5 mins Cook time 10 mins Total time 15 mins

INGREDIENTS

- 1 tablespoon coconut oil
- 2 tablespoons grated ginger
- 2 large cloves garlic, grated
- ½ long red chilli, sliced
- 1 medium celery stick, diced
- 400 g / 0.8 lb. grass-fed ground beef mince
- 2 tablespoons Tamari soy sauce or coconut aminos for soy-free version
- ½ tablespoon fish sauce

- 1½ teaspoon coconut sugar, honey, or ethyritol 'sugar powder for Keto version
- 1 tablespoon sesame oil
- 1 teaspoon tomato paste
- Juice of ½ lime
- 1 tablespoon sesame seeds
- Chopped spring onions/scallions, for garnish
- For cauliflower
- 250-300 g / 0.5 lb. cauliflower (1/2 medium head) florets finely diced into rice-like kernels - you can use a food processor for this
- 1 teaspoon coconut oil, butter or ghee
- Pinch of salt

DIRECTIONS

1. Firstly in a large frying pan, heat coconut oil over medium-high heat. Add the ginger, garlic, chilli, and celery and sauté for 30 seconds, then add the ground beef. Cook for 6 minutes over medium-high heat, breaking the meat apart with a spatula in the first couple of minutes. Then leave the beef to brown off and only stir once or twice.

2. Mix Tamari (or coconut aminos), fish sauce, sweetener of choice, sesame oil, tomato paste, and lime juice in a bowl and beat together. After 6-7 minutes, once the beef has started to brown slightly, add the sauces to the beef and stir through for another minute. Finally, drizzle in the sesame seeds and stir through.

3. While the beef is cooking, heat the oil or butter in another pan over medium-high heat. Add the cauliflower rice and salt and stir through for 1-2 minute, until slightly unstiffened.

4. Serve the beef over cauliflower rice, topped with some chopped spring onions.

2. Easy Beef Tagine

Prep Time: 15 mins Cook Time: 30 mins Total Time: 45 mins Servings: 6 servings Calories: 431kcal

INGREDIENTS

- 2 tablespoons olive oil
- 1 small onion diced
- 2 cloves garlic diced
- 2 pounds beef chuck 1 inch dice
- 2 teaspoons allspice
- 1 1/2 teaspoons red pepper flakes
- 14 ounces crushed tomatoes
- 1/2 cup beef stock
- 6 ounces green olives
- 2 tablespoons preserved lemons
- 7 ounces baby spinach
- 1/3 cup flaked almonds
- 1/4 cup cilantro chopped

DIRECTIONS

1. Firstly place a saucepan over high heat and add the oil, onion, and garlic. Sauté for 3 minutes.

2. Then add the diced beef and sauté until browned.

3. Add the spices, tomatoes and beef stock, seethe for 30-40 minutes until the beef is tender.

4. Combine through the olives and lemon, then take away from the heat.

5. Stir through the spinach, until wilted.

6. Present topped with the almonds and coriander, and with a side of Cauliflower Rice.

3.   Chicken & Goat Cheese Skillet

Total Time Prep/Total Time: 20 min. Makes 2

servings

INGREDIENTS

- 1/2 pound boneless skinless chicken breasts, cut into 1-inch pieces
- 1/4 teaspoon salt
- 1/8 teaspoon pepper
- 2 teaspoons olive oil
- 1 cup cut new asparagus (1-inch pieces)
- 1 garlic clove, minced
- 3 plum tomatoes, chopped
- 3 tablespoons 2% milk
- 2 tablespoons herbed new goat cheddar, disintegrated
- Hot cooked rice or pasta
- Extra goat cheddar, optional

DIRECTIONS

1. Throw chicken with salt and pepper. In a large skillet, heat oil over medium-high heat; sauté chicken until not, at this point pink, 4-6 minutes. Eliminate from dish; keep warm.

2. Add asparagus to skillet; cook and mix over medium-high heat 1 moment. Add garlic; cook and mix 30 seconds. Mix in tomatoes, milk and 2 tablespoons cheddar; cook, covered, over medium heat until cheddar starts to liquefy, 2-3 minutes. Mix in chicken. Present with rice. Whenever wanted, top with extra cheddar.

4. Spicy Tandoori Lamb Meatballs

Servings: 32 + meatballs

INGREDIENTS

- 2 lbs. ground lamb or ground pork, beef or a mixture
- 2 cloves garlic minced
- 1/2 cup chopped fresh cilantro
- 1/4 cup ground chia seed
- 1/4 cup water
- 2 tbsp. coconut aminos or soy sauce
- 1 tbsp. fish sauce use Red Boat for paleo
- 2 tsp. paprika
- 1 1/2 tsp. ground ginger
- 1 1/2 tsp. ground coriander
- 1 1/2 tsp. ground turmeric
- 1 tsp. ground cumin

- 1 tsp. salt
- 1/2 tsp. black pepper
- 1 to 2 teaspoon cayenne pepper depending on how hot you like it
- 3 tbsp. sesame seeds for garnish
- Additional chopped cilantro for garnish

DIRECTIONS

1. Firstly preheat oven to 400F and line a large, rimmed baking sheet with parchment paper.
2. In a large bowl, combine all ingredients except for sesame seeds and combine well.
3. Form into 1 & 1/2 inch balls and put on prepared baking sheet. You should get 32 or more meatballs.
4. Bake 12 to 15 minutes, until browned and cooked through.
5. Remove and drizzle with sesame seeds and additional chopped cilantro.

5. Chicken & Vegetable Penne with Parsley-Walnut Pesto

Active:20 mins Total:30 mins Servings:20

INGREDIENTS

- ¾ cup chopped pecans
- 1 cup daintily stuffed parsley leaves
- 2 cloves garlic, squashed and stripped
- ½ teaspoon in addition to 1/8 teaspoon salt
- ⅛ teaspoon ground pepper
- 2 tablespoons olive oil
- ⅓ cup ground Parmesan cheese
- 1 ½ cups shredded or cut cooked skinless chicken bosom (8 oz.)
- 6 ounces entire wheat penne or fusilli pasta (1 3/4 cups)
- 8 ounces green beans, managed and divided across (2 cups)

- 2 cups cauliflower florets (8 oz.)

DIRECTIONS:

1. Stage 1
2. Heat a huge pot of water to the point of boiling.
3. Stage 2
4. Spot pecans in a little bowl and microwave on High until fragrant and daintily toasted, 2 to 2 1/2 minutes. (On the other hand, toast the pecans in a little dry skillet over medium-low heat, blending continually, until fragrant, 2 to 3 minutes.) Transfer to a plate and let cool. Set 1/4 cup to the side for fixing.
5. Stage 3
6. Consolidate the remaining 1/2 cup pecans, parsley, garlic, salt, and pepper in a food processor. Cycle until the nuts are ground. With the engine running, steadily add oil through the feed tube. Add Parmesan and heartbeat until blended in. Scratch the pesto into a huge bowl. Add chicken.
7. Stage 4

8. Then, cook pasta in the bubbling water for 4 minutes. Add green beans and cauliflower; cover and cook until the pasta is still somewhat firming (practically delicate) and the vegetables are delicate, 5 to 7 minutes more. Prior to depleting, scoop out 3/4 cup of the cooking water and mix it into the pesto-chicken combination to warm it marginally. Channel the pasta and vegetables and add to the pesto-chicken blend. Throw to cover well. Split between 4 pasta bowls and top each presenting with 1 Tbsp. of the held pecans.

6. Hasselback Eggplant Parmesan

Active:25 mins Total:1 hr. 20 mins Servings:5

INGREDIENTS

- 1 cup arranged low-sodium marinara sauce
- 4 little eggplants (around 6 inches in length; 1 3/4 pounds complete)
- 2 tablespoons extra-virgin olive oil in addition to 2 teaspoons, partitioned
- 4 ounces new mozzarella, daintily cut into 12 pieces
- ¼ cup arranged pesto
- ½ cup entire wheat panko breadcrumbs
- 2 tablespoons ground Parmesan cheese
- 1 tablespoon chopped new basil

DIRECTIONS

1. Stage 1
2. Preheat oven to 375 degrees F.
3. Stage 2
4. Spread sauce in a 9-by-13-inch grill safe heating dish. Make across cuts each 1/4 inch along every eggplant, cutting nearly to the base however not right through. Cautiously move the eggplants to the heating dish. Tenderly fan them to open the cuts more extensive. Shower 2 tablespoons oil over the eggplants. Fill the cuts then again with mozzarella and pesto (a few cuts may not be filled). Cover with foil.
5. Stage 3
6. Prepare until the eggplants are delicate, 45 to 55 minutes.
7. Stage 4
8. Join panko, Parmesan and the remaining 2 teaspoons oil in a little bowl. Eliminate the foil and sprinkle the eggplants with the breadcrumb blend.
9. Stage 5
10. Increment the oven temperature to sear. Cook the eggplants on the middle rack until the

garnish is brilliant brown, 2 to 4 minutes. Top with basil. Present with the sauce.

7. Asparagus-Mushroom Frittata

Total Time Prep: 25 min. Bake: 20 min.Makes 8

servings

INGREDIENTS

- 8 large eggs
- 1/2 cup entire milk ricotta cheddar
- 2 tablespoons lemon juice
- 1/2 teaspoon salt
- 1/4 teaspoon pepper
- 1 tablespoon olive oil
- 1 bundle (8 ounces) frozen asparagus lances, defrosted
- 1 large onion, divided and daintily cut
- 1/2 cup finely chopped sweet red or green pepper
- 1/4 cup cut infant Portobello mushrooms

DIRECTIONS

1. Preheat oven to 350°. In a large bowl, whisk eggs, ricotta cheddar, lemon squeeze, salt and pepper. In a 10-in. ovenproof skillet, heat oil over medium heat. Add asparagus, onion, red pepper and mushrooms; cook and mix 6-8 minutes or until onion and pepper is delicate.

2. Eliminate from heat; eliminate asparagus from skillet. Hold eight lances; cut leftover asparagus into 2-in. pieces. Return slice asparagus to skillet; mix in egg combination. Organize held asparagus lances over eggs to take after spokes of a wheel.

3. Heat, revealed, 20-25 minutes or until eggs are totally set. Let stand 5 minutes. Cut into wedges.

8. Easy Hamburger Casserole Recipe

Prep Time 15 mins Cook Time 30 mins Total Time 45 mins

INGREDIENTS

- 1½ pounds ground beef see tips below
- 2 tablespoons olive oil plus more for the pan
- 1 teaspoon onion powder
- 1 teaspoon garlic powder
- 1 teaspoon Dijon mustard
- 1 tablespoon tomato paste sugar-free – see tips below
- ½ teaspoon ground pepper
- 1 teaspoon salt
- 3 eggs
- ½ cup heavy cream
- 1½ cups cheddar grated

- 3 cups green beans canned or frozen – see tips below

DIRECTIONS

1. Oil an 8×8″ baking dish with olive oil and set aside. Preheat your oven to 360°F. Put 1½ pounds ground beef, 1 teaspoon onion powder, 1 teaspoon garlic powder, 1 teaspoon Dijon mustard, 1 tablespoon tomato paste, ½ teaspoon ground pepper, and 1 teaspoon salt in a large bowl. Stir well until mixed.
2. Ground beef and other ingredients in a glass bowl for Keto hamburger casserole
3. Heat 2 tablespoons olive oil in a large skillet. Add the ground beef paste and cook for about 10 minutes, breaking it up as it cooks, until it browns completely.
4. Browning the ground beef in a skillet
5. Add the cooked ground beef mixture to your prepared baking dish in an even layer. Blowout 3 cups canned or frozen green beans over the beef.
6. Green beans on top of beef for Keto casserole recipe

7. In a medium bowl, beat 3 eggs. Add ½ cup heavy cream and a pinch of salt. Evenly pour this mixture over the meat and green beans. Spread 1½ cups grated cheese over the top of the beef and green bean mixture.

8. Adding cheese to Keto casserole recipe

9. Then bake for 20-30 minutes, until the cheese is golden brown. Present, and enjoy!

10. Serving of Keto casserole recipe on a plate with a baking dish of hamburger casserole

11. Notes

12. Mix with ground pork: You can use ground pork in addition to beef for even more flavor. Use a mixture of 1 pound ground beef and 5 ounces ground pork if you would like to use pork.

13. Sugar-free tomato paste: Make sure your tomato paste is sugar-free. You can substitute it with sugar-free ketchup.

14. Using frozen green beans: If using frozen green beans, you do not need to thaw them. They will cook completely when baking the casserole.

15. Other veggies to use: Not a fan of green beans? You can still make this easy Keto

hamburger recipe! Try using cauliflower or broccoli instead. Broccoli is one of our personal favorites!

9. Curry Bowl With Spinach

Prep Time:5 minutes Cook Time:10 minutes Total Time:15 minutes Servings: 4 NET carbs: 4g

INGREDIENTS

- 1 onion sliced
- 2 cloves garlic
- 2 tbsp. curry powder
- 750 g (1.7 lb.) ground/minced beef
- 125 ml (0.5 cups) coconut cream
- 6 cups spinach chopped finely

DIRECTIONS

1. Slightly fry the sliced onion in coconut oil until the onion is cooked and clear.
2. Then add the garlic and curry powder, stir and cook for another minute. Be careful not to allow the garlic to burn.
3. Add the ground/minced beef and endure to stir until thoroughly cooked.
4. Add the coconut cream and stir.
5. At the same time as the curried beef is still simmering in the pan, begin to add the chopped spinach one handful at a time. Stir the spinach through the curried beef so it wilts. Repeat until all the spinach is added.
6. Present the Keto curry in bowls, and enjoy! Garnish with coconut cream (optional).

10. Beef Shawarma Bowl

Yields 4 servings

THE PREPARATION

- Shawarma Beef
- 1 ½ pounds 80/20 ground beef
- 1 tablespoon garlic powder
- 1 tablespoon onion powder
- ½ tablespoon cumin
- ½ tablespoon five spice powder
- ½ tablespoon cayenne pepper
- 1 teaspoon salt
- ½ teaspoon ground black pepper
- 2 tablespoons Greek yogurt
- 2 tablespoons fresh squeezed lemon juice
- 2 tablespoons butter
- Cauliflower Rice
- 455 grams (approx. 16 oz.) cauliflower rice*
- 2 tablespoons light soy sauce

- White Garlic Sauce
- 2 tablespoons garlic powder
- ½ teaspoon onion powder
- 4 tablespoons Greek yogurt
- ½ teaspoon salt
- ½ teaspoon ground black pepper
- 2 tablespoons water
- Red Pepper Sauce
- 1 teaspoon crushed red pepper flakes
- 1 tablespoon sriracha
- 1 tablespoon chili oil **
- 2 tablespoons Greek yogurt
- ½ teaspoon salt
- ½ teaspoon ground black pepper
- Optional toppings include finely sliced cabbage, cucumber, tomatoes, avocado, etc.

The Execution

1. In a bowl, combine the ground beef and shawarma beef spices.
2. In a separate container, combine yogurt and lemon juice. Mix until consistent.

3. Combine beef and yogurt mixture. Combine well until combined and sticky. Set aside in the refrigerator while preparing the sauces.

4. For the white garlic sauce, combine all ingredients in a container. Beat to combine. Add more (or less) water for desired consistency. Transfer to a squeeze bottle or small mason jar. May be refrigerated up to two weeks.

5. Mix together all of the ingredients for the red pepper sauce. Add more (or less) water for desired consistency. Transfer to a squeeze bottle or small mason jar. May be refrigerated up to two weeks.

6. Heat 2 tablespoons of butter in a pan. Add marinated ground beef and sauté until cooked through. Transfer to a bowl and cover with foil to keep hot.

7. Meanwhile, using the same pan used to cook the beef, add cauliflower rice. Combine in the soy sauce. Keep stirring until almost dry.

8. To accumulate, layer cauliflower rice, beef, toppings, and sauces.

11. Easy Moussaka

PREP TIME 20 minutes COOK TIME 40 minutes

TOTAL TIME 1 hour

INGREDIENTS

- 450g minced lamb
- 2-3 tbsp. Olive oil to sauté the aubergine (eggplant)
- 1 small onion, finely chopped
- 70g button mushrooms, finely chopped
- ½ tsp. nutmeg
- 1 aubergine, sliced about 3-4mm thick
- 2 garlic cloves, finely chopped
- ½ tsp. ground cinnamon
- 3 tomatoes, quartered
- 2 tbsp. tomato puree
- 1 ½ cup heavy cream
- 100g cream cheese
- 50g grated parmesan cheese

- 20g grated cheddar to sprinkle on the top
- Freshly ground Salt and Pepper

DIRECTIONS

1. Firstly pre-heat the oven to 180C.
2. Fry the minced lamb until browned. Set the cooked mince aside in your baking dish. Slice your aubergine into 3-4mm thick parts. Then fry the eggplant slices in olive oil in a separate pan in batches and set them aside as well.
3. When you have fried the mince, then fry the onion, mushrooms and garlic together until nicely cooked.
4. Add this to your properly sized oven dish and drizzle with the ground cinnamon.
5. Then add the tomatoes (quartered) and tomato puree to the oven dish and mix well.
6. Now add the cream and cream cheese to a saucepan over medium heat and stir until boiling.
7. Then lessen the heat and add the parmesan and the nutmeg. Stirring well until the parmesan cheese is dissolved and the sauce has thickened sufficiently.

8. Then pour the sauce into the mince and mix well. Garnish with salt and pepper to taste.

9. Then add the aubergine slices to the top of the mince until fully covered. Sprinkle the top with some grated cheddar cheese.

10. Place in the oven at 180C for 40 minutes to cook.

12. Easy Meatloaf Meal

servings: 8 SLICES | prep time: 10 MINS | cook time: 1 HR 5 MINS | total time: 1 HR 15 MINS

INGREDIENTS

- 2 pounds 80/20 Ground beef
- 1 medium Onion, diced
- 2 cups Crushed Pork rinds
- 1 large Egg
- 2 tablespoons Worcestershire sauce
- ½ teaspoon Garlic powder
- 1 teaspoon Salt
- ⅓ cup Reduced sugar ketchup

DIRECTIONS

1. Preheat oven to 350 degrees F.
2. In a large bowl mix all the ingredients except ketchup. Mix ingredients until fully combined.

3. Press ingredients into a parchment paper lined loaf pan.
4. Then bake for 30 minutes. After 30 minutes add ketchup on top and bake for 25-35 minutes more.
5. Remove from oven and let rest for 15 minutes.
6. Enjoy!

13. Low-Carb 30-Minute Greek Herbed Lamb

Prep Time15 minutes Cook Time15 minutes Total Time30 minutes Servings4 Calories714.5kcal

INGREDIENTS

- Lamb
- 1.5 lb. lamb tenderloin (fillet)
- 1 tbsp. extra virgin olive oil
- 1 lemon, juiced (2 tbsp.)
- 1/4 tsp. pepper
- 2 tsp. dried oregano
- 1 tsp. dried parsley
- 2-3 crushed garlic cloves
- Cauliflower Mash
- 2 lb. cauliflower chopped
- 1 cup light single, pouring cream

- 3 cups chicken broth
- 1 oz. unsalted butter chopped
- Himalayan salt

DIRECTIONS

1. Make mash: pour cream and chicken stock into a saucepan and turn on the heat. Break the florets off the cauliflower and chop roughly in half, add to the pan.
2. Then bring to the boil then lower the heat and simmer, covered for 15 mins.
3. Once cauliflower is simmering, make the lamb marinade.
4. Lamb marinade: Mix all the ingredients except the lamb in a small jug and mix to combine.
5. Place lamb in a zip-lock bag and pour over the marinade. Close the bag and wobble the lamb around so it's well coated. Place to marinate for about 10 minutes.
6. Put a fry-pan over medium-high heat and add 1 tbsp. olive oil.
7. Pan-fry the lamb for 3-4 minutes on each side. Rest for a few minutes if time allows.

8. While the lamb is cooking, sewer cauliflower which should be tender by now, reserving 1/4 cup of liquid.

9. Use a food processor or immersion blender to blend the cauliflower, butter, salt and the reserved liquid until pureed.

10. Present the Mediterranean lamb with the cauliflower mash.

14. Corned Beef & Cabbage

YIELDS:6 SERVINGS PREP TIME:0 HOURS 15 MINS

TOTAL TIME:5 HOURS 0 MINS

INGREDIENTS

- 3-4 lbs. corned hamburger
- 2 onions, quartered
- 4 celery stems, quartered transversely
- 1 bundle pickling flavors
- Genuine salt
- Dark pepper
- 1 medium green cabbage, cut into 2" wedges
- 2 carrots, stripped and cut into 2" pieces
- 1/2 c. Dijon mustard
- 2 tbsp. apple juice vinegar
- 1/4 c. mayonnaise
- 2 tbsp. escapades, generally chopped, in addition to 1 tsp. saline solution

- 2 tbsp. parsley, generally chopped

DIRECTIONS

1. Spot corned hamburger, onion, celery, and pickling flavors into a large pot. Add sufficient water to cover by 2", season with salt and pepper, and heat to the point of boiling. Lessen heat to low, cover, and stew until delicate, 3–3 1/2 hours.

2. In the mean time, whisk Dijon mustard and apple juice vinegar in a little bowl and season with salt and pepper. In another bowl, blend mayo, tricks, escapade salt water, and parsley. Season with salt and pepper

3. Add cabbage and carrots and keep on stewing for 45 minutes to 1 hour more, until cabbage is delicate. Eliminate meat, cabbage, and carrots from pot. Cut corned meat and season with more salt and pepper.

4. Present with the two sauces as an afterthought for plunging.

15. Keto Broccoli Salad

YIELDS:4 SERVINGS PREP TIME:0 HOURS 15 MINS

TOTAL TIME:0 HOURS 35 MINS

INGREDIENTS

- FOR THE SALAD
- legitimate salt
- 3 heads broccoli, cut into scaled down pieces
- 1/2 c. shredded Cheddar
- 1/4 red onion, meagerly cut
- 1/4 c. toasted cut almonds
- 3 cuts bacon, cooked and disintegrated
- 2 tbsp. newly chopped chives
- FOR THE DRESSING
- 2/3 c. mayonnaise
- 3 tbsp. apple juice vinegar
- 1 tbsp. Dijon mustard
- Genuine salt

- Newly ground dark pepper

DIRECTIONS

1. In a medium pot or pan, heat 6 cups of salted water to the point of boiling. While trusting that the water will bubble, set up a large bowl with ice water.
2. Add broccoli florets to the bubbling water and cook until delicate, 1 to 2 minutes. Eliminate with an opened spoon and spot in the readied bowl of ice water. At the point when cool, channel florets in a colander.
3. In a medium bowl, race to join dressing ingredients. Season to taste with salt and pepper.
4. Consolidate all serving of mixed greens ingredients in a large amaze and pour dressing. Throw until ingredients are consolidated and completely covered in dressing. Refrigerate until prepared to serve.

16. Chicken Caesar Pasta Salad

Active:20 mins Total:30 mins Servings:16 (according to pan)

INGREDIENTS

- ½ cup low-fat buttermilk
- ¼ cup low-fat plain Greek yogurt
- 3 tablespoons extra-virgin olive oil
- 2 tablespoons new lemon juice
- 2 teaspoons Dijon mustard
- 1 ½ teaspoons anchovy paste
- 1 huge garlic clove
- ¾ cup finely ground Parmesan cheese, separated
- ½ teaspoon salt, separated
- ½ teaspoon ground pepper, separated
- 8 ounces entire wheat penne

- 3 cups shredded cooked chicken bosom
- 1 16 ounces cherry tomatoes, split
- 5 cups chopped romaine lettuce

DIRECTIONS

1. Stage 1
2. Consolidate buttermilk, yogurt, oil, lemon juice, mustard, anchovy paste, garlic, 1/2 cup Parmesan and 1/4 teaspoon each salt and pepper in a blender; puree on fast until smooth, around 1 moment. Put in a safe spot.
3. Stage 2
4. Cook pasta as per bundle directions, overlooking salt. Channel, saving 1 cup cooking water.
5. Stage 3
6. Consolidate the pasta, chicken, tomatoes, 1/4 cup of the saved cooking water and the remaining 1/4 teaspoon each salt and pepper in a huge bowl. Mix in the buttermilk dressing until altogether joined. Mix in extra cooking water depending on the situation for a rich consistency. Cover and chill for at any rate 30 minutes or as long as 2 days.

7. Stage 4

8. Not long prior to serving, mix in lettuce; sprinkle with the remaining 1/4 cup Parmesan.

17. Ground beef meal

Cook Time: 20 minutes | Total Time: 30 minutes

Servings: 6 Calories: 360kcal

INGREDIENTS

- 500 g ground beef (1lb)
- 2 brown onions (sliced)
- 250 g button mushrooms (cut into quarters)
- 2 garlic cloves (minced)
- 1 cup beef stock
- 1 cup sour cream
- 1 tbsp. Dijon mustard
- 6 cups Shirataki noodles (optional)
- to taste salt and pepper
- for cooking oil of preference
- garnish fresh parsley (optional)

DIRECTIONS

1. Firstly in a piping hot pot, add a little bit of oil and the mushrooms and allow the mushroom to get a good sear.

2. Next, add the onion, ground beef and garlic. Season with generously with salt and pepper. Permit the ground beef to brown and the onions to soften. Stirring consistently to prevent burning. About 10 minutes.

3. Next add the Dijon mustard and the beef stock and bring to a boil.

4. Remove from heat a stir in the sour cream. Add salt if needed.

5. Enhance with fresh parsley.

18. Lamb & Beef meal

Active:25 mins Total:40 mins Servings:4

INGREDIENTS

- Ingredient Checklist
- 1 ½ cups water
- 1 cup brown basmati rice
- 8 ounces lean ground beef
- 8 ounces ground lamb
- 3 cups chopped yellow onions
- 2 tablespoons chopped garlic
- 1 tablespoon ground turmeric (see Tip)
- 2 teaspoons grated fresh ginger
- 1 ½ teaspoons ground coriander
- 1 teaspoon ground cumin
- 3 tablespoons tomato paste
- 3 cups unsalted beef broth
- 2 tablespoons Worcestershire sauce

- ¾ teaspoon salt
- ¼ cup low-fat plain Greek yogurt
- 3 tablespoons chopped fresh cilantro

DIRECTIONS

1. Step 1
2. Mix water and rice in a medium saucepan; bring to a boil over high heat. Reduce heat to a simmer, cover and cook until the water is absorbed, about 40 minutes.
3. Step 2
4. Meanwhile, cook beef and lamb in a large skillet over medium-high heat, crumbling with a wooden spoon, until no longer pink, 5 to 6 minutes. Add onions and cook, stirring occasionally, until translucent, 6 to 8 minutes.
5. Step 3
6. Increase heat to high. Add garlic, turmeric, ginger, coriander and cumin; cook, stirring, until fragrant, about 1 minute. Stir in tomato paste and cook, stirring, for 1 minute. Stir in broth, Worcestershire and salt; bring to a boil. Reduce heat to medium and simmer, stirring sporadically, until thickened, 13 to 15 minutes.
7. Step 4

8. Present the meal over the rice, topped with some yogurt and cilantro with naan bread on the side.

19. Shepherd's Pie meal

Servings 8 servings' calories per serving 350kcal prep time: 30 minutes cook time: 30 minutes

INGREDIENTS:

- FILLING
- 1 tbsp. coconut oil
- 1.5 lbs. ground beef/lamb
- 1/2 cup onion, diced
- 2 stalks celery, diced
- 1 large carrot, diced
- 2 cloves garlic, minced
- 1 tsp. rosemary
- 1 tsp. thyme
- 1.5 tsp. pink Himalayan salt
- 1/2 tsp. black pepper
- 1 cup chicken broth
- 2 tbsp. tomato paste
- 1-2 tbsp. Worcestershire sauce

- MASHED CAULIFLOWER TOPPING
- 1 large cauliflower head, cut into small florets, steamed (see video above on how to steam cauliflower)
- 1 cup shredded cheddar cheese
- 2 tbsp. cream cheese, softened
- 2 tbsp. heavy cream
- 2 tbsp. butter, softened
- 2 cloves garlic
- 1/2 tsp. pink Himalayan salt
- 1/4 tsp. black pepper
- fresh parsley, garnish

DIRECTIONS:

1. Firstly heat oil in a large pan over medium-high heat. Add beef (or lamb) and cook until no longer pink, breaking it up with a wooden spoon and stirring recurrently, about 5 minutes.

2. Add cubed onions, celery, carrots, garlic, and seasonings to the pan. Cook until the vegetables soften, about 5 minutes, stirring occasionally.

3. Add broth, tomato paste, and Worcestershire sauce to the pan, stirring until the paste

dissolves. Reduce heat slightly and let it continue to simmer until the sauce thickens, about 15 minutes, before turning off the heat.

4. Preheat oven to 400 degrees F.

5. Place steamed cauliflower to a food processor or blender. Add ½ cup cheddar cheese, cream cheese, cream, butter, garlic, salt, and pepper. Puree until smooth consistency, scraping the sides as necessary (See video above for steps on how to steam the cauliflower).

6. Allocate meat and veggie mixture to a 2-quart baking dish, spreading it in an even layer.

7. Spread the mashed cauliflower evenly over the meat, then top with remaining shredded cheddar cheese.

8. Bake for 30 minutes, or until the peaks of the mashed cauliflower are browned. Remove from oven and cool slightly, then garnish with parsley, if desired. Serve immediately.

20. Asparagus With Hollandaise Sauce

Prep Time: 10 minutes | Cook Time: 5 minutes | Total Time: 15 minutes | Servings: 4 | Calories: 248kcal

INGREDIENTS

- 1 pound asparagus, trimmed
- 1 tablespoon water
- salt and pepper to taste
- Hollandaise Sauce
- 4 ounces salted butter
- 2 large egg yolks
- 1/2 teaspoon Dijon mustard
- 1 tablespoon water

- 1-2 teaspoons freshly squeezed lemon juice (or white vinegar)
- 1-2 pinch cayenne pepper
- 1-2 pinch white pepper

DIRECTIONS

1. If the asparagus is medium to large in wideness, cut 1 inch off of the bottoms and lightly peel the stalks with a vegetable peeler. I start about 1/3 from the top and continue to the bottom of each spear. If the asparagus is thin, hold a spike towards the bottom and bend it until it snaps. Cut the remaining spears to the same length. Discrete the eggs, reserving the whites for another use.

2. Asparagus:

3. Put the asparagus in a microwave safe bowl and add 1 tablespoon of water. Cover with plastic wrap and cook at high power from 1 1/2 - 2 1/2 minutes depending on your microwave. Drain off the water and keep covered. Alternately, blanch the asparagus in boiling water until it is crunchy tender, drain, and keep warm.

4. Blender Hollandaise

5. Add the egg yolks, 1 tablespoon of water, 1 teaspoon of lemon juice and the mustard to a blender. Place the lid on top and remove the middle piece. Place the butter in a medium to large frying pan and melt the butter over medium heat. Turn the heat up to medium high and slightly swirl the pan every few moments. When the solids in the bottom of the pan just begin to turn brown, turn off the heat. Turn the blender on low and begin pouring the hot butter into the blender, leaving the brown solids behind in the pan.

6. After the butter has been incorporated, add the cayenne pepper and white pepper and blend. Taste. Adjust seasoning with more acid, salt or pepper. Pour over the asparagus and serve immediately.

21. Pasta e Fagioli Soup Freezer Pack

Active:15 mins Total:8 hrs. 15 min Servings:6*12

INGREDIENTS

- 2 cups chopped onions
- 1 cup chopped carrots
- 1 cup chopped celery
- 1 pound prepared Meal-Prep Sheet-Pan Chicken Thighs (see related formula), diced
- 4 cups cooked entire wheat rotini pasta
- 6 cups diminished sodium chicken stock
- 4 teaspoons dried Italian flavoring
- ¼ teaspoon salt
- 1 (15 ounce) can no-salt-added white beans, washed
- 4 cups infant spinach (half of a 5-ounce box)
- 4 tablespoons chopped new basil, isolated (Optional)
- 2 tablespoons best-quality extra-virgin olive oil

- ½ cup ground Parmigiano-Reggiano cheese

DIRECTIONS

1. Stage 1
2. Spot onions, carrots and celery in an enormous sealable plastic sack. Spot cooled cooked chicken and cooked pasta together in another pack. Seal the two packs and freeze for as long as 5 days. Thaw out the packs in the fridge short-term prior to continuing.
3. Stage 2
4. Move the vegetable blend to a huge lethargic cooker. Add stock, Italian flavoring and salt. Cover and cook on Low for 7 1/4 hours.
5. Stage 3
6. Add beans, spinach, 2 tablespoons basil, if using, and the thawed out chicken and pasta. Cook for 45 minutes more. Scoop the soup into bowls. Shower a little oil into each bowl and top with cheese and the remaining 2 tablespoons basil, whenever wanted.

22. Easy Pie Meatballs

Total time : 40 minutes Outcome : 6 servings

Cooking time : 25 minutes

INGREDIENTS

- To prepare the meatballs :
- 1 pound ground meat (80/20)
- 1 pound of ground lamb
- 1 / 2 cup almond flour peeled
- 2 eggs
- 1 tablespoon of Worcestershire sauce
- 1 tablespoon finely grated carrot
- 1 teaspoon fresh thyme leaves
- 1 / 2 teaspoon garlic powder
- 1 / 2 teaspoon onion powder
- 2 teaspoons kosher salt
- 1 / 2 tsp. crushed black pepper
- 2 tablespoons olive oil, for frying
- To prepare the sauce :
- 1 tablespoon of tomato paste

- 1 1/2 tablespoons Worcestershire sauce
- 1 1/4 cup chicken broth
- 1 / 2 teaspoon kosher salt
- 1 / 2 teaspoon of mustard powder
- 1 / 4 teaspoon black pepper
- 1 / 4 teaspoon of xanthan gum

DIRECTIONS

1. To make meatballs :
2. Firstly place all of the meatball ingredients (except oil) in a medium bowl . Mix it well with your hands, then shape into 18 meatballs about 5 cm in diameter . Heat the oil in a large non-stick frying pan over a medium heat for two minutes, or until the oil is glistening. Add the meatballs and cook for 3 minutes, then turn them over with tongs and cook for another 3 minutes or until golden brown . Eliminate the meatballs from the pan and set aside .
3. To prepare the sauce :
4. Add all sauce ingredients to the same frying pan where you cooked the meatballs and stir well . Bring the sauce to a boil over a high heat, then reduce the heat to medium and

return the meatballs to the skillet and stir well through the sauce . Simmer the paste on low heat for 10 minutes, or until it thickens and reduces by about a third and the meatballs are cooked . Present warm, preferably over a Keto Cheddar Leek Cauliflower Mash.

5. Store leftovers in an airtight container in the refrigerator for up to 5 days or in the refrigerator for up to 3 months .

23. Budget Beef Meal Prep

PREP TIME: 15 MINUTES COOK TIME: 30 MINUTES

TOTAL TIME: 45 MINUTES SERVINGS: 5

INGREDIENTS

- FOR THE BEEF:
- 2 pounds ground beef
- 2 teaspoons each fresh parsley & mint chopped
- 1.5 teaspoons each smoked paprika & cumin
- ¼ teaspoon cayenne pepper
- 2 cloves garlic grated
- ½ teaspoon dried thyme
- Zest of ½ a lemon
- Kosher salt & black pepper
- Avocado or grape seed oil
- FOR THE YOGURT SAUCE:
- ¾ cup full fat Greek yogurt
- 1 teaspoon each fresh parsley & mint chopped

- Zest of half a lemon
- 1 tablespoon lemon juice
- 1 clove garlic
- 1 teaspoon extra virgin olive oil
- Kosher salt & black pepper
- FOR THE PILAF:
- 2 medium size zucchini about 12 ounces
- ½ a head of cauliflower
- 1 pound of broccoli with stalks or 12 ounces of florets
- ½ an onion chopped
- 2 cloves garlic minced
- 1 teaspoon mustard seeds
- ¼ teaspoon red pepper flakes
- 1 teaspoon each fresh parsley & mint chopped
- Zest and juice of half a lemon
- 2 tablespoons chopped pecans roasted if desired
- Kosher salt & black pepper
- Avocado or grape seed oil

DIRECTIONS

1. Cook's notes: Watch the video in this post to see how to cut the zucchini, cauliflower, and broccoli for the pilaf. Everything is cut small and similar in size, so they cook evenly.

2. Firstly make the pilaf by chopping the zucchini, cauliflower, and broccoli into small parts that are roughly the same size, making sure not to use too much of the stalks. Pre-heat a large and wide pan over medium heat for 2 minutes. Add 2 teaspoons of oil to the pan and then the onions, garlic, mustard seeds, red pepper flakes, ¼ teaspoon salt, and a couple cracks of pepper. Mix well and cook for 6 minutes, stirring often. Add the sliced zucchini, cauliflower, and broccoli to the pan along with ½ teaspoon of salt and a few cracks of pepper. Combine well and place a lid on the pan, you can also use a sheet tray to cover the pot if you don't have a lid. Cook for 10-12 minutes, stirring a few times. The veggies are ready when they have softened up, but still have a bite to them. Turn the heat off the pan and add the parsley, mint, lemon zest and juice, and pecans, mix well. Check for seasoning, you

may need more lemon juice or salt. Set it aside.

3. For the beef kefta, add the ground beef to a large bowl along with the remaining elements (not the oil), 1 teaspoon of salt, and a few cracks of pepper. Use your hands to mix everything very well. Form the kefta by taking a little of the meat and shaping it like log or football,. You will have enough beef to make 14-15 kefta. Pre-heat a large pan, preferably cast iron over medium-high heat for 2 minutes. Add 2 teaspoons of oil to the pan, wait 30 seconds so the oil can heat up, then add half the kefta to the pan. Cook for 3-4 minutes, or until well browned, flip and cook another 3-4 minutes. Once both parts are browned, you may need to cook the kefta on the sides for 30 seconds to cook them all the way through. If you are not sure the kefta are done, cut one in half and check, it's significant not to overcook the kefta otherwise they will dry out. Remove kefta from pan, add a little more oil, and cook the second batch. While the kefta are cooking, make the yogurt sauce by combining

everything in a bowl and whisking well. Check for seasoning and amend if needed.

4. Present the kefta with some yogurt sauce and pilaf, enjoy! Everything will keep in the fridge for 5 days, you can freeze the kefta for 2-3 months, but I would not recommend freezing the veggies as they will get very soft and watery. The best way to reheat the kefta and veggies is in a 400 F oven for 10 minutes, if using a microwave, cover the container with a wet paper towel and make sure not to overheat, as the beef will dry out.

24. Low Carb Turkey And Peppers

PREP TIME: 20 MINUTES COOK TIME: 15 MINUTES

TOTAL TIME: 20 MINUTES YIELD: 4 SERVINGS

INGREDIENTS

- 1 teaspoon salt, isolated
- 1 pound turkey tenderloin, cut into slight steaks about ¼-inch thick
- 2 tablespoons extra-virgin olive oil, isolated
- ½ large sweet onion, cut
- 1 red ringer pepper, cut into strips
- 1 yellow ringer pepper, cut into strips
- ½ teaspoon Italian flavoring
- ¼ teaspoon ground dark pepper
- 2 teaspoons red wine vinegar
- 1 14-ounce can squashed tomatoes, ideally fire-cooked

- Chopped new parsley and basil for decorate (optional)

DIRECTIONS

1. Sprinkle ½ teaspoon salt over turkey. Heat 1 tablespoon oil in a large non-stick skillet over medium high heat. Add half of the turkey and cook, until browned on the last, 1 to 3 minutes. Flip and keep cooking until cooked completely through, 1 to 2 minutes. Eliminate the turkey to a plate with an opened spatula, tent with foil to keep warm. Add the excess 1 tablespoon oil to the skillet, diminish heat to medium and rehash with the leftover turkey, 1 to 3 minutes for every side.

2. Add onion, chime peppers and the leftover ½ teaspoon salt to the skillet, cover and cook, eliminating top to mix frequently, until the onion and peppers are relaxing and brown in spots, 5 to 7 minutes.

3. Eliminate top, increment heat to medium high, sprinkle with Italian flavoring and pepper and cook, blending regularly until the spices are fragrant, around 30 seconds. Add vinegar, and cook, mixing until totally dissipated, around 20

seconds. Add tomatoes and bring to a stew, blending regularly.

4. Add the turkey to the skillet with any amassed juices from the plate and bring to a stew. Diminish heat to medium-low and cook, turning in the sauce until the turkey is hot entirely through, 1 to 2 minutes. Serve finished off with parsley and basil if using.

25. Dijon Salmon with Green Bean Pilaf

Total:30 mins Servings:6 (more according to time)

INGREDIENTS

- 1 ¼ pounds wild salmon (see Tip), cleaned and cut into 4 bits
- 3 tablespoons extra-virgin olive oil, isolated
- 1 tablespoon minced garlic
- ¾ teaspoon salt
- 2 tablespoons mayonnaise
- 2 teaspoons entire grain mustard
- ½ teaspoon ground pepper, isolated
- 12 ounces pretrimmed haricots verts or slender green beans, cut into thirds
- 1 little lemon, zested and cut into 4 wedges
- 2 tablespoons pine nuts
- 1 8-ounce bundle precooked brown rice
- 2 tablespoons water
- Chopped new parsley for decorate

DIRECTIONS

1. Stage 1
2. Preheat oven to 425 degrees F. Line a rimmed heating sheet with foil or material paper.
3. Stage 2
4. Brush salmon with 1 tablespoon oil and spot on the readied preparing sheet. Pound garlic and salt into a paste with the side of a gourmet expert's blade or a fork. Consolidate an insufficient 1 teaspoon of the garlic paste in a little bowl with mayonnaise, mustard and 1/4 teaspoon pepper. Spread the combination on top of the fish.
5. Stage 3
6. Cook the salmon until it pieces effectively with a fork in the thickest section, 6 to 8 minutes for every inch of thickness.
7. Stage 4
8. Then, heat the remaining 2 tablespoons oil in a huge skillet over medium-high heat. Add green beans, lemon zing, pine nuts, the remaining garlic paste and 1/4 teaspoon pepper; cook, blending, until the beans are simply delicate, 2 to 4 minutes. Diminish heat to medium. Add

rice and water and cook, blending, until hot, 2
to 3 minutes more.

9. Stage 5

10. Sprinkle the salmon with parsley, whenever
wanted, and present with the green bean pilaf
and lemon wedges.

26. Beef and broccoli

Preparation time : 10 Cooking time : 25 minutes

Total time : 35 minutes Number of meals : Calories :

294 kcal

INGREDIENTS

- pound steak, sliced 1/4 inch thick
- 5 cups of baby broccoli florets are about 7 ounces
- 1 tablespoon avocado oil
- To prepare the sauce :
- 1 yellow onion, sliced
- 1 tablespoon butter
- Half a spoonful of olive oil
- 1 / 3 cup of low - sodium soy sauce
- ½ cup beef broth
- 1 tablespoon of finely chopped fresh ginger
- 2 cloves of garlic, finely chopped

DIRECTIONS

1. Heat avocado oil in a skillet over medium heat for a few minutes or until warm . Add beef strips and cook until brown, under 5 minutes, do not stir too much, as they want to brown . Put it on a plate and set aside . Add onions to a frying pan with butter and olive oil and cook for 20 minutes until the onions are caramelized and soft .

2. Add all of the other sauce ingredients to the skillet and stir together over a medium heat until they begin to boil for about 5 minutes . Use a hand mixer to mix the sauce . Keep the sauce warm over low heat and add broccoli to the skillet .

3. Return the meat to the skillet and sauté the broccoli and sauce . Stir until covered with sauce . Bring to a boil and cook for a few more minutes until broccoli is soft . Season with salt and pepper if needed .

4. Serve immediately, perhaps with boiled cauliflower rice .

5. feed

27. Coconut Curry Cauliflower Soup with Toasted Pepitas

YIELDS:4 PREP TIME:0 HOURS 5 MINS TOTAL TIME:0 HOURS 35 MINS

INGREDIENTS

- 1/4 c. pepitas, toasted
- 1 tsp. Additional virgin olive oil
- 2 garlic cloves, chopped
- 1 tsp. new ginger, stripped and chopped
- 1 c. yellow onion, chopped
- 1 c. carrots, chopped
- 1 tsp. legitimate salt
- 1 huge cauliflower head, cut into florets
- 32 oz. low-sodium vegetable stock

- 1 c. full-fat coconut milk (shake well ahead of time)
- 2 tbsp. red curry paste
- 1/4 c. new cilantro, chopped
- Flaky ocean salt

DIRECTIONS

1. In a little skillet, dry toast pepitas on low heat until brilliant brown, around 2 minutes. Put in a safe spot.
2. In an enormous pot over medium-low heat, heat olive oil. Add garlic, ginger, onion, carrots, and salt. Cook for 5 minutes.
3. Add cauliflower, stock, coconut milk, and curry paste. Mix well, heat to the point of boiling, and afterward stew for 20 minutes. Mix with a drenching blender until smooth.
4. Embellish with toasted pepitas, cilantro, and flaky ocean salt. Serve right away.

28. Chicken & Spring Vegetable Tortellini Salad

Active: 30 mins Total: 30 mins Servings: 16+

INGREDIENTS

- 1 pound boneless, skinless chicken bosom
- 2 sound leaves
- 6 cups water
- 1 (20 ounce) bundle new cheese tortellini
- ½ cup peas, new or frozen
- ¼ cup velvety serving of mixed greens dressing, like farm or peppercorn
- 2 tablespoons red-wine vinegar
- 5 tablespoons chopped new spices, like basil, dill and additionally chives, isolated
- ½ cup chopped marinated artichokes in addition to 2 tablespoons marinade, partitioned
- ½ cup julienned radishes

- 1 cup pea shoots or infant arugula
- 2 tablespoons sunflower seeds

DIRECTIONS

1. Stage 1
2. Join chicken, narrows leaves and water in a huge saucepan. Heat to the point of boiling over high heat. Decrease heat to low, cover and stew until a moment read thermometer embedded in the thickest part enlists 165 degrees F, 10 to 12 minutes. Move the chicken to a spotless slicing board to cool.
3. Stage 2
4. Eliminate the narrows leaves. Add tortellini to the pot and return the water to a bubble; cook, mixing incidentally, until the tortellini are simply delicate, around 3 minutes. Add peas and cook brief more. Channel and flush with cold water.
5. Stage 3
6. Then, consolidate dressing, vinegar, 3 tablespoons spices and artichoke marinade in a huge bowl. Shred the chicken and add to the dressing alongside the tortellini, peas, artichokes, radishes and pea shoots (or

arugula); mix to consolidate. Serve the plate of mixed greens finished off with the remaining 2 tablespoons spices and sunflower seeds.

29. Italian Style Meatballs

Prep Time: 15 minutes | Cook Time: 20 minutes | Total Time: 35 minutes | Servings: 4 | Calories: 387kcal

INGREDIENTS

- 1/2 pound ground beef chuck, 85 % lean
- 1/2 pound ground pork (or turkey or veal)
- 1/4 cup Parmesan cheese, grated
- 1/4 cup heavy cream
- 1 large egg, beaten
- 2 tbsp. minced fresh parsley
- 1 tbsp. finely grated onion (it will be mush)
- 1 clove garlic, grated (small - medium in size)
- 1/2 tsp. salt
- 1/4 tsp. pepper

- Optional: Sauce
- 2 cups Rao's Marinara Sauce (or your favorite low carb sauce)

DIRECTIONS

1. Firstly add the beef and pork to a medium bowl and break up into little chunks, aiming for an even mix.
2. Add the remaining ingredients to the meat and mix with a hand mixer until just combined. Do not over-combine.
3. Slightly oil hands and roll 12 meatballs. I weigh mine to get the weights equal for even cooking. To do it by eye, divide the meatball mixture in half and roll 6 meatballs of even looking size and repeat with the remaining meat.
4. To Pan Fry Meatballs:
5. Heat a large frying pan over medium heat. I use a Green Pan, but an iron skillet or stainless steel pan will do (they will need more oil). When hot, spray the pan with oil (use 2 teaspoons for iron or stainless). Add the meatballs to the pan, making sure they each have their own place. [DO NOT crowd the pan.

If your pan is small and you add all of the meatballs, they will steam and be tough. If your pan is large, you can fit all 12 in the pan.]

6. Then cook the meatballs approximately 1 1/2 minutes per side, turning at least 4 times. I use tongs to gently roll them over. Cook for 10-15 minutes total. They should be browned like the picture in the post.

7. Heat the sauce in the pan, scraping up the brown bits for a full flavored sauce. For a fresher tasting sauce, warm on the stove or in the microwave and pour over the meatballs. Enhance with parsley and serve or top with mozzarella cheese and place under the broiler to melt.

8. To Bake Meatballs in the Oven:

9. Firstly pre-heat oven to 400 degrees F and position rack to the middle. Place meatballs on a foil-lined or rack-lined baking sheet. Bake meatballs for 15-20 minutes. Present   with warmed sauce and garnish with chopped fresh parsley. Alternately, top with mozzarella cheese and place under broiler to melt the cheese.

30. Zucchini-Crusted Pizza

Total Time Prep: 20 min. Bake: 25 min. Makes 6 servings

INGREDIENTS

- 2 large eggs, gently beaten
- 2 cups shredded zucchini (around 1-1/2 medium), pressed dry
- 1/2 cup shredded part-skim mozzarella cheddar
- 1/2 cup ground Parmesan cheddar
- 1/4 cup universally handy flour
- 1 tablespoon olive oil
- 1 tablespoon minced new basil
- 1 teaspoon minced new thyme

Fixings:

- 1 container (12 ounces) broiled sweet red peppers, julienned
- 1 cup shredded part-skim mozzarella cheddar
- 1/2 cup cut turkey pepperoni

DIRECTIONS

1. Preheat oven to 450°. Blend the initial 8 ingredients; move to a 12-in. pizza container covered liberally with cooking splash. Spread combination to a 11-in. circle.

2. Heat until light brilliant brown, 13-16 minutes. Lessen oven setting to 400°. Add garnishes. Prepare until cheddar is dissolved, 10-12 minutes longer.

31. Creamy Dijon Chicken

Total Time Prep/Total Time: 25 min. Makes 4

servings

INGREDIENTS

- 1/2 cup creamer cream
- 1/4 cup Dijon mustard
- 1 tablespoon brown sugar
- 4 boneless skinless chicken bosom parts (6 ounces each)
- 1/4 teaspoon salt
- 1/4 teaspoon pepper
- 2 teaspoons olive oil
- 2 teaspoons spread
- 1 little onion, divided and daintily cut
- Minced new parsley

DIRECTIONS

1. Whisk together cream, mustard and brown sugar. Pound chicken breasts with a meat hammer to even thickness; sprinkle with salt and pepper.

2. In a large skillet, heat oil and spread over medium-high heat; brown chicken on the two sides. Decrease heat to medium. Add onion and cream combination; heat to the point of boiling. Decrease heat; stew, covered, until a thermometer embedded in chicken peruses 165°, 10-12 minutes. Sprinkle with parsley.

32. Naked Fish Tacos

Total Time Prep/Total Time: 25 min. Makes 2

servings

INGREDIENTS

- 1 cup coleslaw blend
- 1/4 cup chopped new cilantro
- 1 green onion, cut
- 1 teaspoon chopped cultivated jalapeno pepper
- 4 teaspoons canola oil, separated
- 2 teaspoons lime juice
- 1/2 teaspoon ground cumin
- 1/2 teaspoon salt, separated
- 1/4 teaspoon pepper, separated
- 2 tilapia filets (6 ounces each)
- 1/2 medium ready avocado, stripped and cut

DIRECTIONS

1. Spot the initial 4 ingredients in a bowl; throw with 2 teaspoons oil, lime juice, cumin, 1/4 teaspoon salt and 1/8 teaspoon pepper. Refrigerate until serving.

2. Wipe filets off with paper towels; sprinkle with the leftover salt and pepper. In a large nonstick skillet, heat remaining oil over medium-high heat; cook tilapia until fish simply starts to chip effectively with a fork, 3-4 minutes for every side. Top with slaw and avocado.

33. Balsamic Zucchini Sauté

Total Time Prep/Total Time: 20 min. Makes 4

servings

INGREDIENTS

- 1 tablespoon olive oil
- 3 medium zucchini, cut into dainty cuts
- 1/2 cup chopped sweet onion
- 1/2 teaspoon salt
- 1/2 teaspoon dried rosemary, squashed
- 1/4 teaspoon pepper
- 2 tablespoons balsamic vinegar
- 1/3 cup disintegrated feta cheddar

DIRECTIONS

1. In a large skillet, heat oil over medium-high heat; sauté zucchini and onion until fresh delicate, 6-8 minutes. Mix in flavors. Add vinegar; cook and mix 2 minutes. Top with cheddar.

34. Mediterranean Chicken Quinoa Bowl

Total: 30 mins Servings: 4

INGREDIENTS

- 1 pound boneless, skinless chicken breasts, managed
- ¼ teaspoon salt
- ¼ teaspoon ground pepper
- 1 7-ounce container cooked red peppers, washed
- ¼ cup fragmented almonds
- 4 tablespoons extra-virgin olive oil, partitioned
- 1 little clove garlic, squashed
- 1 teaspoon paprika
- ½ teaspoon ground cumin
- ¼ teaspoon squashed red pepper (Optional)
- 2 cups cooked quinoa

- ¼ cup pitted Kalamata olives, chopped
- ¼ cup finely chopped red onion
- 1 cup diced cucumber
- ¼ cup disintegrated feta cheese
- 2 tablespoons finely chopped new parsley

DIRECTIONS

1. Stage 1
2. Position a rack in upper third of oven; preheat grill to high. Line a rimmed heating sheet with foil.
3. Stage 2
4. Sprinkle chicken with salt and pepper and spot on the readied preparing sheet. Sear, turning once, until a moment read thermometer embedded in the thickest part peruses 165 degrees F, 14 to 18 minutes. Move the chicken to a perfect cutting board and cut or shred.
5. Stage 3
6. Then, place peppers, almonds, 2 tablespoons oil, garlic, paprika, cumin and squashed red pepper (if using) in a scaled down food processor. Puree until genuinely smooth.
7. Stage 4

8. Join quinoa, olives, red onion and the remaining 2 tablespoons oil in a medium bowl.

9. Stage 5

10. To serve, partition the quinoa blend among 4 dishes and top with equivalent measures of cucumber, the chicken and the red pepper sauce. Sprinkle with feta and parsley.

35. Fish Fillets with Vegetable Sticks

Prep time: 20 min Serving 3

INGREDIENTS

- 4 halibut or other firm-fleshed white fish fillets (total 11/2 lb./750 g)
- 2 tbsp. low-sodium soy sauce
- 2 tbsp. white wine or sake
- 1 small knob peeled fresh ginger minced
- 2 medium carrots cut into long matchsticks
- 2 oz. snow peas cut in halves lengthwise
- 1/2 yellow bell pepper

DIRECTIONS

1. Firstly Place fillets in a small, shallow baking dish that will fit inside a large, deep skillet. In a small bowl, stir together soy sauce and wine. Put over fish. Top with ginger and carrots; set aside.

2. Now Fill skillet with about an inch of water. Bring to a simmer. Place a wire rack in the skillet.

3. Place baking dish containing the fish on the wire rack, and cover. Steam these for five to six minutes.

4. Add snow peas and yellow pepper to the baking dish and again cover it. Steam until fish flakes when touched with a fork and vegetables are crisp-tender, about five minutes. Present immediately.

36. Asian chicken

Prep: 5 mins Cook: 8 mins , serving: 8

- CHICKEN:
- 500g/1lb breast filets, skinless and boneless (2 huge) (Note 1 different cuts)
- 1/2 tsp. each salt and pepper
- 1 1/2 tbsp. rice flour, or universally handy/plain flour (Note 2)
- 1 1/2 tbsp. oil , vegetable or canola
- SAUCE:
- 2 tsp. sesame oil

- 2 garlic cloves , finely minced
- 1 tsp. bean stew chips/red pepper pieces (decrease for less fiery)
- 1/2 cup water
- 3 tbsp. sriracha (sub ketchup for not fiery, Note 3)
- 1 tbsp. soy sauce , light or universally handy (Note 4)
- 1/4 cup nectar (sub brown sugar)
- 3 tbsp. lime juice (sub 2 tbsp. rice vinegar)
- Enhancements (CHOOSE):
- Green onion (finely cut), sesame seeds, new stew, lime wedges

DIRECTIONS:

1. CHICKEN:
2. Season: Cut every chicken bosom fifty-fifty on a level plane to frame 4 steaks absolute. Sprinkle each side with salt, pepper and rice flour, shaking off overabundance.
3. Sear: Heat oil in a huge skillet over high heat. Add chicken and cook for 2 minutes. Turn and cook the opposite side for 2 minutes, at that point eliminate to a plate.
4. Tacky Chili SAUCE:

5. Sesame oil: Allow the skillet to cool somewhat then re-visitation of the oven on medium. Add sesame oil and heat.

6. Garlic and ginger: Add garlic and ginger, cook for 15 seconds.

7. Bean stews chips: Add stew pieces and cook for 30 seconds until garlic is brilliant.

8. Sriracha, soy and nectar: Turn heat up to medium-high. Add water, sriracha, soy sauce and nectar, mix well, scratching the base of the dish to break down every one of the brilliant pieces into the fluid.

9. Stew for 2 minutes until it decrease to a thick syrup. Add lime juice, at that point stew for a further 30 seconds until it thickens back to thick syrup.

10. Coat chicken: Turn heat off. Return chicken to dish, going to cover in sauce.

11. Serve chicken, finishing off with residual sauce in skillet, embellished with green onions, sesame seed and additional lime wedges, whenever wanted.

12. Formula Notes:

13. Chicken – Boneless and skinless thighs and tenderloins additionally work, utilize 500g/1lb. Try not to slice down the middle, utilize entire pieces.

14. Thighs will take more time to cook through, around 4 minutes on the primary side, 3 minutes on the subsequent side;

15. Tenderloins are (commonly) more modest so they should take the around a similar time as bosom.

16. Inside temperature of cooked chicken:

17. Bosom and tenderloin: 65°C/150°F

18. Thigh: 75°C/167°F

19. Rice flour – Yields a decent, firm outside layer onto which the tacky stew sauce sticks. Without it, the sauce simply sneaks off the chicken. It is anything but a serious deal in the event that you don't have it – sub plain/generally useful flour. Rice flour is simply somewhat crisper. ☺

20. Sriracha – This adds fieriness just as different flavors like vinegar and garlic into the sauce, in addition to it thickens the sauce.

21. On the off chance that you need less zesty, sub some of it with ketchup. In the event that you sub every last bit of it, the dish turns out to be very sweet so add a scramble of additional lime to redress (it's likewise absolutely not what this formula is proposed to be, but rather it's as yet delicious!)

22. In the event that you need fiery however don't have sriracha, additionally sub with ketchup in addition to some other hot sauce to taste, or cayenne pepper or more stew chips.

23. Soy sauce – Use universally handy or light, don't utilize dim soy sauce (shading and flavor excessively extraordinary). More on various soy sauces here.

24. Capacity – Lean meats like bosom and tenderloin are in every case best served newly made. However, it will save for 3 – 4 days in the cooler. Best to reheat in the microwave, and delicately, so you don't overcook it!

Conclusion

I would like to thank you all for choosing this book. Hope you all liked the best meals recipes. These recipes are suitable for certain hypertension patients and these will urge you to lessen the sodium in your eating routine and eat an assortment of food sources wealthy in supplements that help lower pulse, like potassium, calcium and magnesium and also help in weight reduction. These recipes will help you in making delicious meals at home also. Prepare for yourself, your family members and appreciate. Good luck!

CPSIA information can be obtained
at www.ICGtesting.com
Printed in the USA
BVHW051725120521
607127BV00003B/708